JOHN WEDGWOOD CLARKE

SEA SWIM

VP

VALLEY
PRESS

First published 2012 by Valley Press
Woodend, The Crescent, Scarborough, YO11 2PW
www.valleypressuk.com

ISBN 978 1 908853 06 6
Cat. no. VP0029

Cover photo: Lara Goodband

1 3 5 7 9 8 6 4 2

A CIP catalogue record for this book is available from the British Library.

Printed and bound in Great Britain by Imprint Digital, Upton Pyne, Exeter.

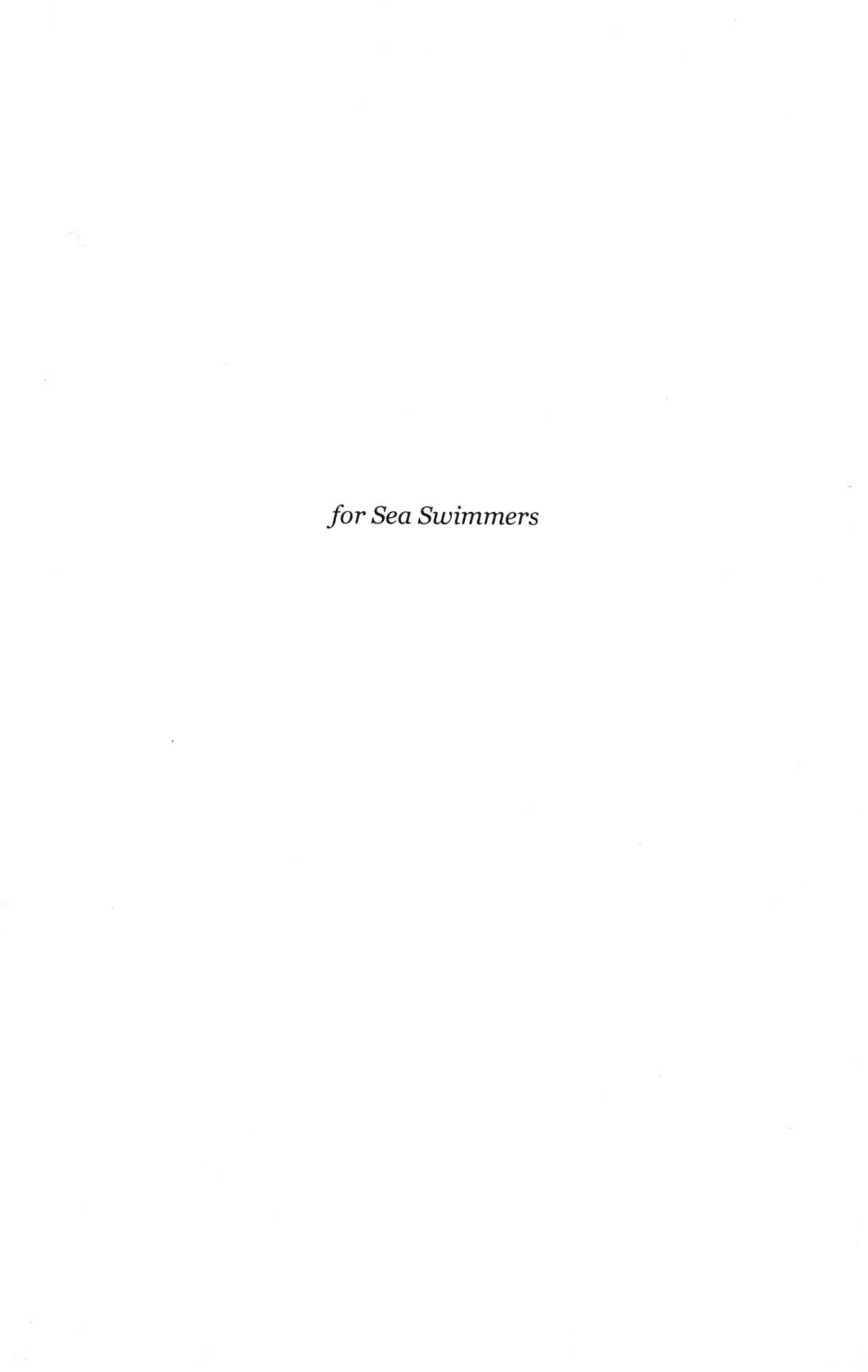

for Sea Swimmers

Contents

South Bay: 12.30-13.00, 26.09.2011

Your wake complicates mine.
Our footprints dream in the tide.

One way, a castle, Ferris wheel, lighthouse,
the Grand Hotel all brick mirage –

the other, a Jurassic cliff's
crumbling book of the unwritten.

Waves hold us as they have held sight before.
Terns hunt eels as if we were not here.

Rings

A quiet migration of swimmers,
stroke, splash and ripple –
where we were going didn't matter;
there was my wedding ring
reaching under water,
a man surfacing in his dark wetsuit,
like a cormorant, further out,
and two Norman windows
of the ruined castle –
here I am, I thought, here I am again.

Beach chalets

are small wooden stanzas
in which words undress
and step from the damp
boards and sixty-watt bulbs
into colossal light,
blinking, rubbing arms,
lifting a little on their toes
as if trying to see over the cold,

ready as they will never be
for the body to speak itself again
for the first time
in the mouth of the North Sea,
the body like a bell note
struck by an iron key,
wordless in a furl of murk,
weed, someone's foot,

and up, shouting, turnstones
overhead, the Hispaniola
rocking by, treading water
back into now, rooted
in all the strange words –
children, parents –
in hands that have held
and let go, swimmers in song.

Hand

Ragged waves – the sea
breaks threads

shoddy daylight
lank and unravelling.

Open silence
and close on it:

a child's sodden glove –
moss on the wall.

Rain Swim

How everywhere it comes at once dissolves its entrance –
the fog unburdens in light so even
we cannot see the drops that make the sea spring up
forests of elastic stalagmites.

How the world turns through us – our bodies floating
off record, needle-poised now there's
nothing to utter other than tinny fizz
shifting everywhere in, filling the horizon with here.

Warship, South Bay

Its outline catches, slipping thoughtful grey
over grey: obelisk and sphere, blind box
and covered deck – steely secrets
we swim towards, the North Sea ablaze over
naked hands, eyes like barnacles
snatching at sight in the easterly spray,
the hut we've left no more than a photo
tugged from a wallet and propped on a rock.
It has suddenly caught up with us
now that we've cut ourselves out of routine,
this curiously unbranded (but for
a tiny red flag like a pilot fish) celebrity
without makeup, a gantry's spiderweb
flawing its hull as the sun hollows through.

Hydro

I still have the M&S shorts with the chain-link
pattern you wore when you balanced me there,
a wild glass of water in the corner
of that outdoor pool, light's brilliant wires
skipping through themselves, my shadow
a frisky amoeba blundering in another world.

We swim between ourselves

in a place never ours; what words we have
for who we are, call from the sea wall –
even the rocks are noisy as they breathe
in the stillness, whispering of tides and rivers.

Repeat the move of a splitting seed –
geese barrel over from Holbeck to Sandside,
memory a flicker of turnstones
lifting and landing as the swimmers return.

Landing

Voices at sea: warm chirrup, chequered shell –
bright things silvering in, out, a missed
word heard as the sound of you tucked in
crush of air, accumulated falling
waves jostling cauliflower lit glass pearl prinking

mussel fragments among stones – this scouring
veil through which breath spans and lands
toeholds in us, sand falling away and lifted
to any foot, your foot, filled with – *I feel*
she calls out, *where* [twists of air] *I'm meant to be.*

Swimming Lesson

Let him imagine some small object
is placed in the water just out of reach
and let him struggle to reach it;
the more he reaches the faster he will swim.
The Art of Swimming, Captain Webb

Let the swimmer imagine
an apple, a feather,
a salver wobbling out of sight,
their father's stubble,
the way she hummed that song;
the name of a field, an alley
where they hid, a blue
stone in the shape of a heart,
a tin-foil galleon;
a raindrop, a snowfall, fish
resisting the barbs
of a lure, a kiss, the first
night of lost earrings...
reach for them –
perfect your stroke
as you reach beyond reach.

Polystyrene

An onshore wind launches blocks
back up the beach, gusts of white milt
skipping in the driven sand, clots
of full stops conspiring in the corner
by the lifeboat house, the wind undecided.

Captain Webb at Scarborough Aquarium

The intense concentration of self in the middle
of such heartless intensity, my God! who can tell it?
Moby Dick, Herman Melville

1. *'Living Death'*

The man on the matchbox who swam The Channel
floated in a tank for seventy-four hours
where now there's an underground car park.
They pushed toast out to him on a tray;
he drank tea for an encore. He was not
booked again, unlike Little Louis *with her powers*
of second sight; for who knew this was a man
drowning under the weight of an empire?
So the story flowed on to its end at Niagara,
the corpse identified by his famous red shorts.

2. Pip

The camera's a dark horizon and the sea
ignorant of another itch in its surface.
There is nowhere to look but look back
and then to the back of beyond
where the day forgets its going on and reverberates,
a silent bell tightening its wound
round your mouth. Seventy-four seconds –
a second for each hour, in memory
of all those times when you could not bear
the way the sky pumped the treadle
of your fear. How much of your body there is
between start and finish, how many
smiles fail in the face of the horizon
as the sea homes in with brilliant insects.

Acrobats

We swim without end, entertaining no one
in shadows beneath us, new capes of light
breaking over our hands, human-headed islands
calling across archipelagos of wake.

Water happens about our ears, laughing
because laughter in the pleasure of another
is the way we know we're together
as Angie dives again, her legs like Breughel's *Icarus*.

Swimmers' Way

Voices, cold wetsuits, salt-sticky towels,
hearts dropped from teapots,
cakes crumbed, sand swept
and out past the sea rose

laden with children and bees,
down through the shelter,
its white growths, kelp slack as road kill,
a voice shouting *glass!*

concrete steps smoothed into ripples
where they pour into sand
and the swimmers step
out of the town and deeper into

here through the entrance
of waves, un-housed life
heading for the sun on the old man
in his yellow rowing boat,

for the shadow's edge, immense,
intimate and streaming
from hands as they dive between sun
and the cold shift of cliffs.

A stunning

head-butt through the plate-glass
curve of January –
waves more like vices

bracing the skull while the sky
unscrews a bright cry
from the head's

unclamped dictionary
of shock and flood – ice-cubes
welded to retinas,

horizons flung
back into distance, away from
blood-berg and melt,

the eyes' dry pebbles
dropping through a rock pool.

Continuous Waterway

We meet in other hands
our shapes in the sea
each migrant movement
borderline of touch

undone in the wind in waves
the moon in tides
where no one plants a flag
without a cage

Winter Minutes

souls are exhaled from moist things
Heraclitus

The sea has chilled and cockled this book.
Words migrate through its pages:
both doors of the chalet are open; the horizon
a lightly tapped tuning fork.

There's nothing to record but your absence.
A tiny spider, auburn-legged, light
as sea foam, sews along the table's aluminium edge.
I write *in absentia*, snow on the sea.

John Wedgwood Clarke trained as an actor at the Guildhall School of Music and Drama and holds a D.Phil. in Modernist poetics from the University of York. He is currently Leverhulme Artist in Residence at the Centre for Environmental and Marine Sciences at the University of Hull, Scarborough. He is UK and Ireland poetry editor for Arc Publications and teaches poetry on the part-time creative writing degree at the University of Hull. He grew up in St. Ives, Cornwall, and now lives and swims in Scarborough.

His poems have appeared in various publications and competitions. In 2010 he was shortlisted for the Manchester Poetry Prize. *'His work is amongst the best to have emerged from new poets in this country over the past two or three years.'* Simon Armitage